Royal Doulton Series Ware

Volume 5

New Discoveries

LOUISE IRVINE

RICHARD DENNIS
1998

ROYAL DOULTON SERIES WARE

Print, Design and Reproduction by Flaydemouse, Yeovil, England
Production by Wendy Wort
Published and distributed by Richard Dennis,
The Old Chapel, Shepton Beauchamp, Somerset TA19 0LE

ISBN 0 903685 53 1

© 1998 Richard Dennis and Louise Irvine

Cover: Pattern book drawing for the Arabian Nights series, D3420.

Acknowledgements

We wish to thank the following enthusiasts for sending us the
information in this volume: M. Barber, S. Baynton, D. Beard,
R. Berlyn, C. Biernacki, D. Billings, D. Blackburn, W. Calcott,
Cantabrian Antiques, E. Coultard, A. Cross, Daphne's Antiques,
F. Dearden, C. Delameter, J. Duckett, A. Edwards, L. & G. Fiterstein,
D. Goodes, S. Green, B. Harris, M. & B. Hayton, M. Herbstman,
B. Hill, S. Holt, J. Iannantuoni, P. Jackman, E. Jacobsen, J. Jenkins,
P. & T. Kester, L. Kramer, B. Lenton, E. Lineham, J. Lukins, V. McIver
E. Nevell, S. Nunn, Phillips Auctioneers, D. Pinchin, M. Plutae, N. Poole,
J. Post, T. Power, J. Reid, W. Richards, V. & L. Roberts, H. Rosenthall,
H. Rothberg, K. Saunders, B. Schreiber, M. Short, J. Smith, H. Speed,
C. & N. Spencer, D. Stevens, P. Stevenson, G. Ternes, G. Tromans,
N.Tzimas, P. Wagner, L. Walker, B. Waller, C. Watts, E. Wetzork,
V. Wingham, B. Zak. Our thanks also to Alexander Clement,
Julie McKeown and Sandra Baddeley of Royal Doulton for providing
photographs and information from the company archives.

We hope readers and collectors will continue to send Louise Irvine
information on new discoveries.
R.D. 1998

Contents

How to use this book

This volume features many of the scenes discovered by collectors and dealers since the publication of *Royal Doulton Series Ware Volumes 1-4*. The new information is classified by volume and each series appears in alphabetical order together with its original page reference. Some unusual new shapes have been recorded but the listings are not comprehensive as the variety of shapes used on Series ware is so extensive. The Shape Guide at the end of Volume 1 gives an indication of the most typical Series ware shapes and can help with identification. However, collectors should expect to find unrecorded shapes as a matter of course. Different ways of collecting Series ware are discussed in the introduction and some interesting collections are illustrated.

Collection of *Dutch - Harlem* ware.

Collecting Series Ware

LOUISE IRVINE

When the first book on Series ware was published in 1980, most pieces could be picked up for very modest prices. Today, the London salerooms report record results for items that previously would not have justified individual cataloguing. Although the prices realised for rare series, such as *Early Motoring* and *Golfing*, might seem daunting to new collectors, there is still plenty of scope for beginning an interesting and affordable collection. There are around three hundred different series, with a vast assortment of shapes dating from the early 1900s, and many interesting themes to explore.

For book lovers there is a wide range of literary subjects, including *Dickens* ware which is one of the most popular series. Early English literature is represented by schoolroom classics, such as Chaucer's *Canterbury Tales* and the various *Shakespeare* series, whilst American readers might enjoy looking out for examples from the *Hiawatha* or the *Rip Van Winkle* series. One of the longest running literary series was *Under the Greenwood Tree*, featuring the exploits of Robin Hood and his Merry Men, which was produced between 1914 and 1967 and is avidly collected on both sides of the Atlantic.

In some cases the Series ware designs can be linked to original book illustrations, which adds a new dimension to browsing in antiquarian book shops. In others, Art Director Charles Noke has perused the pages of his favourite novels or plays and visualised his own scenes. One of his most successful series was the *Jackdaw of Rheims*, which was widely promoted in Doulton literature of the early 1900s and produced in both china and earthenware. The tale of the jackdaw who stole the Cardinal's ring, was written by Thomas Ingoldsby (pen name of Richard Harris Barham) and was a popular music hall recital in Victorian times. Noke has recreated all the incidents in this absurd story as if they were taking place behind an ivy-clad stone wall and his designs appeal greatly to collectors today. These are just a few of the subjects from literature; the choice is wide and varied if the aim is to form a 'library' Series ware collection inspired by different books.

For those who prefer fact to fiction, a colourful pageant of British history is enacted on Series ware, from the Norman Conquest illustrated on the *Bayeux Tapestry* series, to the Victory commemoratives for World War One. Series such as *Historic England* and *Historic Towns* depict famous characters with important national landmarks, whilst other aspects of the country's rich architectural heritage are illustrated on the *Castles and Churches* series or *Old English Inns*. It could be fun to commemorate an enjoyable touring holiday of Britain with a souvenir Series ware collection inspired by different books.

Included in such a souvenir display might be some traditional thatched cottages along with many other idyllic rustic views seen through Charles Noke's rose-coloured spectacles. His romantic vision created an Olde Worlde England populated with knights in shining armour, jovial monks, country bumpkins and elegant ladies of leisure, all of which make colourful Series ware subjects. One of the most collected series in this category is *Coaching Days*, which was in production for fifty years and is to be found enhancing oak dressers all over the world. The choice of shapes in this series is enormous but so far only one moustache cup has been reported making this a very rare item.

Scenes of hunting, shooting and fishing, the great British field sports, were also very popular subjects, particularly overseas, as they epitomised the lifestyle of the landed classes, which many wealthy Americans adopted. For those opposed to blood sports, however, there

Collection of teapot stands, tea caddies, sugar sifters and small vases.

Collection of teapot stands.

are many scenes of animals in happier circumstances, including the comic dogs of the great British illustrator, Cecil Aldin, and the satirical cats of Australian cartoonist David Henry Souter.

Cartoon characters were also ideal subjects for nursery wares as were fairy tales and nursery rhymes and these are now sought after by those of a nostalgic nature. Many of these children's series are the hardest of all to find as they did not survive the rough and tumble of nursery life. Series depicting Victorian and Edwardian children at play are also very appealing, the most desirable being *Blue Children*, which features romantic sylvan scenes with angelic girls and boys, immaculately dressed in frilled bonnets and smocks or velvet knickerbockers. More children, of the kind that were seen but not heard, are to be found in the scenes inspired by the work of Kate Greenaway, the Queen of the English nursery, but these are frustratingly elusive today.

The subjects discussed so far are very English but there is also scope for patriotic overseas collectors to acquire pieces relating to their own history and traditions in the extensive selection of scenes from around the world. Australian collectors are particularly well served as Royal Doulton's first agent 'down under', John Shorter, commissioned a succession of designs featuring wattle and waratahs, koalas and kangaroos. However, there are also series depicting subjects from America, Canada, South Africa and New Zealand.

Series ware subjects are many and various but even more wide-ranging are the shapes available. Most collectors find the rack plates easiest to display and collections of two hundred plus are not unknown. Others like to seek out every conceivable shape in their chosen series and the most commonly found are illustrated in the shape guide at the end of *Royal Doulton Series Ware* Volume 1. This list does not claim to be comprehensive and new discoveries are being made all the time. Amongst the most interesting are the early metal-mounted pieces which appear on the market occasionally, for example the sugar sifters, jam pots, cruet sets and tankards with ornate pewter lids. Several decanter barrels, incorporating metal fittings, have been sold in recent years but less familiar will be the cocktail shaker which has been recorded in Caldecott's *Hunting*, the *Golfing* and the *Coaching* series.

Coaching Days biscuit barrel.

Caldecott cocktail shaker.

Welsh and *Teatime Sayings* tea caddies.

Above: *Bluebell Gatherers* sugar sifter.

Left: *Caldecott* decanter barrel.

Coaching Days and *Under the Greenwood Tree* mustard pots.

Dickens cruet set.

Perhaps one of the rarest Series ware shapes is the shaving mug and to date only *Aldin Dogs, Dickens, Old Moreton Hall* and *Shakespeare* scenes are known. In contrast, matching Series ware toilet sets were plentiful in Edwardian times but were highly prone to damage during daily use. In any event they are unlikely to be collected in any number today because of space constraints. Nevertheless, the appearance of unusual accessories, like slop buckets, create a lot of interest and are priced accordingly. Matching chamber pots are hard to find should a collection of this nature be considered. The idea is not unique as at least one English inn is known to hang chamber pots from the rafters. An equally bizarre taste in interior decoration can be seen at the Prince Regent pub in Marylebone High Street, London, where cheese dishes are attached to the walls above the diners. So far no Doulton examples are to be seen there so perhaps the proprietors would be interested to hear of the extensive Series ware range, including the unusual *Witches* cheese dish in a previously unrecorded shape.

Gaffers sugar sifter.

Gondoliers marmalade jar.

Gallant Fishers (Izaak Walton) sugar sifter.

Desert Scenes cheese dish.

No matter how unusual an idea may seem, there will be collectors somewhere. There is, for instance, a society for hatpin stand collectors and the Doulton Series ware examples are much in demand amongst their members. An American collector is currently researching a book on cookie jars, or biscuit barrels as they are known in England, and was fascinated to learn that there are lots of Series ware types. These biscuit containers are often confused with tobacco jars and here again there is an extensive Series ware selection as illustrated by a London collector who has managed to find more than fifty different designs. As there is not a definitive list for this or any other Series ware shape, collectors have no way of knowing whether their search is nearing completion but fortunately the mystery element is part of the fun of collecting – who knows what will turn up next!

Gleaners and Gypsies, Countryside and *Sir Roger de Coverley* hatpin stands.

Collection of teapots and rack plates.

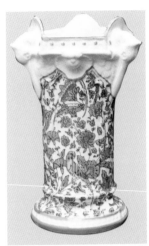

Persian vase.

Dickens biscuit barrel.

Countryside chamber pot.

Left: *Music* and *Dance* umbrella stand; right: *Greek* spittoon.

Bateman, Old English Inns, Under the Greenwood Tree and *Sedan Chair* pin trays.

Canterbury Tales vase and *Arabian Nights* jug.

It was this seemingly limitless scope that appealed to the American teapot collector. So far she has tracked down eighty examples including several previously unrecorded shapes. Series ware teacups and saucers would also make an attractive collection and a highlight of such a display might be one of the party sets, which were made with extra space on the saucer to hold cake or sandwiches. To date these sets have only been recorded in the *Gibson* and *Nightwatchman* series. Another teatime shape, which was not previously listed, is the tea caddy and this was made in designs such as *Old Moreton Hall* and *Peter Pan*.

A collection of tea caddies, party sets, cocktails shakers or even chamber pots would take a very long time to amass so it is probably best to concentrate on the more obvious shapes which are usually the most accessible. Series ware steins or jugs were made in a variety of different patterns and can create an effective and cohesive display as indeed can ashtrays or, for the non-smoker, pin trays. One London collector has been quietly seeking out these little trays at very affordable prices and she now has around fifty examples. Part of their appeal, from her point of view, is that they feature a wide assortment of the illustrative Series ware backstamps. They also have the advantage of being uniform in shape and compact for display purposes, criteria which apply equally to miniature Series wares. However, Lilliputian vases and jugs were discovered by collectors many years ago and now command very high prices. More than fifty different patterns and a wide selection of tiny vases, jugs, teapots and mugs have been recorded. One of the rarest miniature shapes is the small promotional plaque which was given to retailers who sold Series ware in the early 1900s and is known in the *Dickens* and *Gaffers* patterns.

Series ware is obviously a vast, varied and sometimes expensive subject but this should not deter enterprising collectors from identifying a personal, affordable niche in the market and building a fascinating collection. Happy hunting!

Unusual *Dickens* promotional plaque mounted in silver frame with hallmark for 1925.

Dickens musical cigarette box.

15

Collection featuring tobacco jars and decanter barrels.

Collection of miniatures.

Nightwatchman party set.

Dickens miniature coffee pot.

Volume 1

Arabian Nights (p13)
A new scene has been discovered which is a variation of Ali Baba's Return, (scene 4). A publicity photograph showing a wide range of shapes has come to light.

Robert Burns (p14)
A bulb bowl has been found featuring scene 2, 'A Cottage Home', which was previously only illustrated from the pattern books.

Beggars Opera (p14)
A blue and white jug has been found in this series, dated 1936.

Dickens (p20)

Publicity photograph showing a wide range of shapes has come to light.

Dickens (p20)

Group A: Uriah Heep, character 28, can be found on rack plates with and without a desk beside him.

Mr. Mantalini, character 31, has been discovered on a rack plate. He has also been found with a different background on a jug shape 6061 (not illustrated).

Dickens (p25)
Group B: A photograph of scene 3, featuring the Artful Dodger and Oliver Twist on a loving cup, is now available.

Group C: A photograph of scene 3, featuring Tony Weller on a jug, is now available.

Group E: An illustration of Bill Sykes modelled in low relief on a jug is now available.

Dickens (p26)
Group D: Mr. Micawber and Mr. Pickwick have been found on plates with a gold art deco border.

Diversions of Uncle Toby (p30)
A new scene has been discovered on a Regent flower bowl.
Another pattern number has also been recorded, D3161.

A teacup has been found featuring Golf,
scene 5.

Don Quixote (p32)
'The fight with the giants'
scene has been discovered
on a tobacco jar and
polychrome plate with fruit
and blossom border
(not ilustrated).

An unrecorded jug has been
found depicting scene 10
Football, which was not
illustrated previously.

The series described as
Don Quixote B is actually
King Arthur's Knights,
pattern number D3120.

Gallant Fishers
[Izaak Walton] (p34)
A new pattern number, D2680, has been
recorded on a biscuit barrel.
Pattern number D3680 is Gallant Fishers
(Volume 2 p127, not illustrated).

Gulliver's Travels (p37)
A blue and white plate has been discovered with the scene 'The poor man squalled terribly' surrounded by a scroll and flower border. A Becket jug has been discovered with the scene 'I lay in great uneasiness' and 'The Binding'.

Jackdaw of Rheims (p38)
A publicity photograph showing a wide range of shapes has come to light.

Rip Van Winkle (p40)

Scene 6, 'Eying him from head to foot with great curiosity', has now been found on a plate and a Hecla jug.

Shakespeare (p44)

Group A: A plate has been found depicting scene 6 *The Tempest*. Mira: 'Sweet Lord you play me false'.

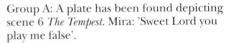

Shakespeare (p45)

Group B: Shakespeare's Plays
A plate, D3199, has been found depicting scene B9 but inscribed *The Tempest* Act 1 Scene Pro: 'The hour's now come; The very minute bids thee ope thine ear. Obey, and be attentive. Canst thou remember a time before we came unto this cell? I do not think thou wast not out three years old'. Mira: 'Certainly, Sir I can.' Group B scenes have also been found on plaques, 13 inches (33cm) in diameter, with a plain band border.

Group D: Shakespearean Knights
A jug, D1978, has been found depicting Sir John Falstaff with the quotation 'A tapster is a good trade' (not illustrated).

Shakespeare (p49)
Group F:
*A Midsummer
Night's Dream*
A new character,
Starveling, has
been found on a
Hecla jug.

A new pattern
number, D3984,
has been recorded
in this series
(not illustrated).

Shakespeare (p51)
Group G: Shakespearean Characters in appropriate
settings. This series continued longer than originally
thought and was produced on bone china plates with
a gilt border until the late 1930s. Hamlet (G5) is
illustrated.

The backgrounds sometimes vary
in this series. Hamlet (G5) is shown
against a curtain background
rather than the woods.

An unfinished
plate shows
Rosalind
without a
background.

Group G:
A new pattern number, D3876, has been
recorded on a tray (not illustrated).

Shakespeare (p53)
Group I: Shakespeare's Country
Several new scenes have been recorded in
this series: Warwick Castle on a Corinth jug;
Maxstoke Castle, (not illustrated).

Under the Greenwood Tree [Robin Hood] (p57)

A new pattern number, D5623, has been recorded on a plaque with oak leaves border, (not illustrated). Publicity photographs showing a wide range of shapes have come to light.

Under the Greenwood Tree [Robin Hood]

Willow Pattern Story (p59)
A new pattern number has been recorded on a tea plate, E7211, which brings the introduction date of this series forward to 1913 (not illustrated).

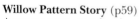

Aldin – Old English Scenes (p63)
A Leeds oval fruit bowl and a Cheshire cheese dish have been found with scene 6 showing two country folk outside an inn.

Aldin's Dogs (p63)

A Celadon plate has been found depicting a dog smoking a pipe surrounded by other dogs.

A rare shaving mug has been discovered in this series.

Bateman (p63)

A jug depicting the officer has been discovered and pin trays featuring the laughing caddies.

The card game (scene 10) is titled 'The Revoke' (not illustrated).

Bradley (p64)

Will Bradley died in 1862.
Group A: This series is taken from his publication *Beauty and the Beast*. Characters A4 and A11 have been found on a rack plate.

Bradley (p67)

Group C: Proverbs. A new proverb has been recorded, 'Marry in haste, repent at leisure. Happy is the wooing that is long in the doing' (not illustrated).

Caldecott (p70)
Our Haymaking
Two plates with
a checkered
border have
been found
depicting The
Tedding (scene
16) and The
Carrying (scene
17).

A Hunting Family (p70)
A rack plate has been discovered depicting
scene 19. Scenes 18 and 20 have been found on
an unusual cocktail shaker, a decanter barrel, a
biscuit barrel and a rack plate.

Souter (p78)
Group B: The quotation for scene 6 is 'Pussy cat, pussy cat where have you wandered'.

A vase has been found with a row of dead mice forming a frieze at the top.

Authors and Inns (p81)
Photographs of jugs featuring Chaucer at 'Ye Tabard Southwark', (scene 1); Goldsmith at 'Ye Rosemary Branch Inn' (scene 2), and The Queen's Head, Islington' (scene 4) are now available. The Castle Inn, Marlborough, and the Roebuck Inn, Knebworth, have also been recorded. It is possible that these scenes divide into two different series. The Queen's Head, the Castle Inn and the Roebuck Inn all feature verses by Shenstone but no portraits of authors.

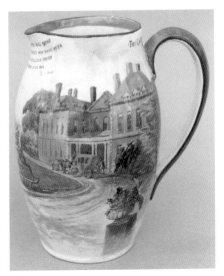

Bayeux Tapestry (p82)
A publicity photograph showing a wide
range of shapes has come to light.

Castles and Churches (p83)
New pattern numbers have been recorded for a large plaque, diameter 15ins (38cm), depicting Pembroke Castle, D5686; for a plate depicting Rochester Castle, D3610, (not illustrated); and for a plate depicting Hurstmonceaux Caste, D4504 (not illustrated).

Salisbury Cathedral has been recorded on a Holbein jug, D2654 (not illustrated).

The pattern number for Croydon Church, D2654, has now been found on a Ball teapot and a Brisley jug (not illustrated).

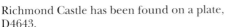

Ardencapel Castle has been found on a York sandwich tray, D4643.

Richmond Castle has been found on a plate, D4643.

Dryburgh Abbey has been found on vase number 7502.

Dover Castle has been found on a Quorn jug, D4643.

31

Famous Sailing Ships (p86)
Two different views have been found of HMS
Victory and East Indiaman (not illustrated).

Historic Towns (p87)
Cambridge – A Leeds fruit bowl has been
found featuring scenes from Cambridge:
Kings and Clare College from the Backs; Old
Court, Trinity College and the Bridge of
Sighs, St. John's College.

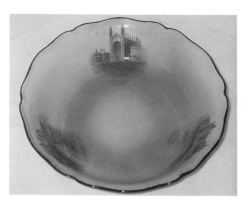

Historic Towns (p88)
Group A: Old London
Two miniature vases have been
discovered in this series. One
depicts 'Izaak Walton, A bit of old
Fleet Street', 'Izaak Walton House,
Fleet Street', and 'Near Izaak
Walton's House. The other depicts
'On the Thames by the Tower',
'Traitor's Gate', 'Beauchamp and
Devereaux Tower' and 'Part of the
Tower of London'.

Historic Towns (p91)

Group E: Old Winchester
New scenes have been found: The Trusty Servant, The Great Screen, and King Alfred's Statue, plus a new pattern number, D3147.

Canterbury
A vase has been found featuring Westgate Cathedral, Augustine's Abbey and Weavers (not illustrated).

Chester
A plate has been found featuring St. John's Priory, Chester.

Hastings and Battle
Two bowls have been found featuring the Gateway, Battle Abbey and Old Houses, All Saints St., Hastings.

Historic Towns (p91)

Ipswich
An ashtray has been discovered with a scene of the Post Office and Town Hall, Ipswich, D3647.

Lincoln
A vase has been found featuring the Roman Gate at Lincoln and the Lincoln Imp (not illustrated).

Historic England (p93)
A pin tray featuring a thatched cottage has been found in this series, possibly Mary Arden's Cottage.

Dr Johnson (p93)
A new scene inscribed 'A Cup of Tea with Dr Johnson' has been recorded on a Joan teapot.

Nautical History A (p94)
The scene recorded as the 'Battle of Trafalgar' has also been founded marked 'Battle of the Nile' and another scene entirely has been discovered marked 'Battle of Trafalgar'.

Another plate has been recorded featuring Commodore Macdonough's Victory. Battle of Plattsburgh Sep 11, 1814. Commissioned by The Tuttle and Pashall Co, Platsburgh, NY, Sole Importers 1913, (not illustrated).

Battle of Trafalgar.

Battle of the Nile.

Old English Inns (p96)
A publicity photograph showing a wide range of shapes has been found.
The Roebuck Inn at Knebworth has been discovered in this series, (not illustrated).

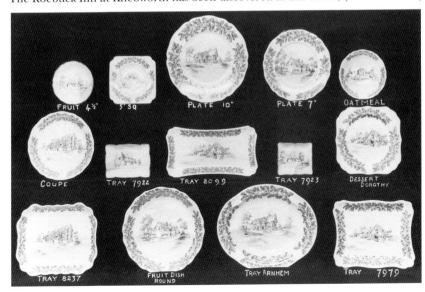

Old Moreton Hall (p97)
This series has also been recorded in
translucent china, TC1031.

A bulb bowl has been found featuring the
Squire and his Lady (scene 2) and a man in
the stocks.

A rare shaving mug has been found
featuring scene 7.

Volume 2

King Arthur's Knights or Tournament (p13)

Two jugs have been found depicting scenes 1, 5, 6 and 7, which were illustrated previously by pattern book illustrations. A publicity photograph showing a wide range of shapes has come to light.

Monks (p16)
Group B: A jug has now been found in this
series with characters 3, 5 and 6.

Monks (p17)
Group C: A stein, D4451, has been found in
this series which was illustrated previously
from the pattern books.

Monks and Mottoes (p18)
Group C: A Ball cream jug, sugar bowl and
teapot have now been discovered in this series.

Monks in the Cellar (p18)
A plate has been found with the scallop shell
and scroll border.

New Cavaliers (p20)
The facsimile signature of Charles Noke has
been recorded on this series.

A new drinking
character has been
found on an
unusual jug.

Characters 6 and 10, previously
illustrated from the pattern books,
have now been found on a plate.

Characters 7, 5 and 9
have been found all
together on several
shapes. Many new
shapes have been
discovered including: a
Baron jug in three
different sizes (left);
a Clent jug in three
different sizes(below)
with hunting silhouette
border;
(continued overleaf)

New Cavaliers (p20)
(continued)
a Mayfair toilet set
and slop bucket; a
7227 candlestick;
square and round pin
trays; several
unrecorded shapes
including jugs; a salad
bowl and a square
moulded plate.

Two of the mottoes found on some shapes
have now been recorded 'Better so than
worse' and 'Ever drink ever dry'(not
illustrated).

Nightwatchman (p21)
An unusual plate has been found in Whieldon ware with a border of lanterns and stars.

Bartolozzi Etchings (p33)
A new series featuring engravings by Francesco Bartolozzi has been noted. This Italian artist came to England in 1764 and reproduced many pictures from the Royal collection. He made stipple engraving fashionable and his work introduced paintings by Angelica Kauffman, Sir Joshua Reynolds and others to a wider audience. The scenes include Master Philip Yorke by Reynolds and three portraits of ladies.

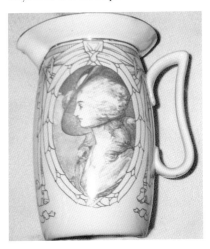

Professionals (p25)
The Squire has been recorded in two different colours and borders, the earlier one has a red coat, the later one a green coat. In the early series of Professionals, the Mayor usually wears a red hat and in the later series a black one (not illustrated).

Toasting Mottoes A (p28)
The missing quotation has now been recorded, 'Take fortune as you find her. And if she frowns don't you'. The Tavern jugs have been found in three sizes.

Chivalry (p35)
Scenes 3 and 5 have now
been photographed on a
plate and jug. A publicity
leaflet has been found.

Kensington Gardens (p38)
A plate has now been found
depicting scene 5 which was
illustrated previously from a
pattern book.

Sedan Chair (p43)
Two new scenes have been discovered on plates: one shows a lady in a sedan chair with the attendants standing to attention; the other shows the attendants ready to lift the sedan chair. Incidental characters also appear on a pin tray (see p14).

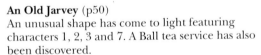

Teatime Sayings B (p45)
Another pattern number, D3609, has been recorded on a Clive teapot which now dates the series introduction to 1912.

An Old Jarvey (p50)
An unusual shape has come to light featuring characters 1, 2, 3 and 7. A Ball tea service has also been discovered.

Coaching Days (p52)

Three new scenes have been discovered on a cup, saucer and dish: a passenger with two bags and a youth with buckets; a passenger and a country yokel; a huntsman at ease on his horse (not illustrated).

Scenes 3, 4 and 16 are now illustrated on actual pieces rather than pattern book photographs.

An unusual image has been found on the reverse of a cup featuring scene 16. A fragment of a damaged lithograph makes it appear as if a lady is buried in the snow!

Coaching Days (p52)
A Rex mug has been discovered with a
duelling scene in the same style as this series.

A very rare moustache mug has been
discovered in this series.

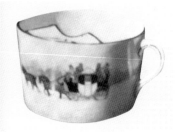

Royal Mail Coach (p59)
A toilet set has been found featuring
several of the scenes previously only
recorded from the pattern books.

Galleons (p61)
Scenes 4 and 5, previously illustrated from the
pattern books, have now been found on a jug.

Ships A (p69)
An ashtray, number 7710, has been found
with a new scene and pattern number,
D2592.

Bluebell Gatherers (p72)
A publicity photograph showing a wide range of shapes has come to light.

The Cottage Door
An entirely new scene has been found on a plate, D3617, showing a family at tea outside a cottage with a stately home in the distance.

A publicity leaflet has been found entitled English Garden.

Country Garden (p77)
A new scene has been found on a teapot showing a young woman gathering flowers.

Country Sayings (p78)
A stein has been discovered with a new character and inscription 'They who won't be counselled can't be helped'.

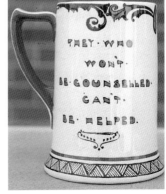

Countryside (p80)
A new scene has been
discovered on a Breda teapot.

Countryside (p80)
A Concord jug has been found featuring
scene 1 previously illustrated from the
pattern books.

Another scene, featuring three cottages, has
been found on a plate (not illustrated).

Elderly Farmworkers (p80)
A Stroon jug has been found featuring an
old man with a rake which was illustrated
previously from the pattern books. It
features the motto 'He hath most who
coveteth least'.

English Cottages (p81)

Group A: There appear to be two different styles of decoration in this group. Pattern number D4390 includes scenes 1 and 2 and these have deep blue skies and broadly painted cottages. A new scene has been found on a square plate.

Pattern number D4987 includes scenes 3-6 printed against a pale blue sky with finely detailed trees and other features in the landscapes. Scene 5 has now been found on a fruit bowl and three new cottage scenes have been discovered on fruit dishes and bowls.

A new pattern number, D3668, has also been recorded on a Simon jug and a sandwich tray and this discovery dates the introduction of this series to 1913 (not illustrated).

English Cottages (p81)

A publicity leaflet has been found, D4987.

Gleaners and Gypsies (p89)
A teapot has been found with a new scene featuring an old woman and a boy.

Illustrated Proverbs (p92)
This series should be known as 'English Proverbs Illustrated' and a new scene has been recorded 'Fine feathers make fine birds' (not illustrated). A jug featuring scene 3 'Fast bind, fast find' has now been photographed.

50

**Plough Horses –
Silhouette** (p95)
A blue and white
tobacco jar has been
found in this series
with the inscription
'He who will calmly
smoke will think like a
sage and act like a
samaritan' (not
illustrated).

"PLOUGHING"

ROYAL DOULTON
POTTERIES
BURSLEM
STOKE-ON-TRENT

Ploughing (p97)
A publicity leaflet has been found.

Romany (p98)
Another scene has been recorded in this
series featuring a man and woman round a
campfire with two caravans (not illustrated).
A publicity leaflet has been found.

Rural Churches (p99)
A new scene has been found on a sugar
bowl.

51

Rustic England (p99) A musical cigarette box which plays Grainger's English Country Garden, has been found in this series (not illustrated). A publicity photograph showing a wide range of shapes has been found.

Springtime (p101) A publicity leaflet has been found.

Witches (p105) Scene 1 has been found on an unusual cheese dish with Shakespeare's Dogberry Watch procession on the inside.

Woodland (p105)
New scenes have been recorded on a York
sandwich tray, Tudor jug, round salad bowl
and Leeds fruit dish.

A publicity photograph
showing a wide range of
shapes has been found.

53

Falconry (p108)
A publicity photograph showing a wide range of shapes has been found.

Fox Hunting - relief (p112)
A new scene has been discovered on a jug, showing a huntsman about to jump a fence.

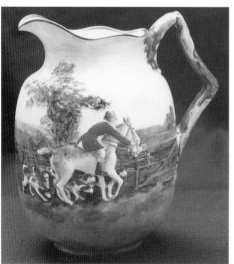

Another new scene on a plate shows a huntsman throwing a rabbit into the air for the hounds.

Hunting B (p115)
Scene 1 is digging out the fox, not a fireside scene (not illustrated).

Hunting - John Peel (p117)
A new scene has been found on a flower bowl which is the same as the Quorn Hunt, scene 5.

Hunting - Morland (p118)
A Flagon toilet set has been found depicting scene 10, previously recorded from a pattern book illustration.

Hunting - Simpson (p124)
Scene 16 is called 'Moving Off' and the late additions to the series are called 'The Old Hound' and 'The Vixen'. New scenes are featured on this cigarette box and ash trays.

Hunting - Thomson A (p125)
A plate has now been found featuring scene 1 of this series, The Meet.

Golf (p129)

Character group 7 has been found on a biscuit barrel and also on a tobacco jar with the inscription 'He that complains is never pitied' (not illustrated).

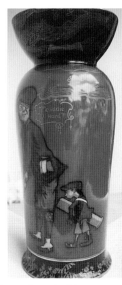

An umbrella stand has been found with a new comic golfing scene, featured in the archives as pattern number D1566 which was introduced in 1902. One side features a golfer about to swing with his caddy beside him and the inscription 'Says Caddie "Hit hard"'. The other side shows the golfer with a broken club and the caddy lying on the ground with the inscription 'Hard hit'.

Character group 7 has also been found on an unusual candlestick, shape 7519.

Character group 6, which was previously illustrated from the pattern books, has been found on a vase and jug.

Old English Country Fairs (p132)
An unusual cheese dish has been found featuring scene 5, the wheelbarrow race.

Skating (p136)
Several new scenes and characters have been found on an unusual pair of vases and a pair of candlesticks.

Sporting Scenes (p138)
'The Benevolent Sportsman' scene 2, has been found on plates
with completely different decorative treatments.

Surfing (p139)
This scene was inspired by Kiama Beach, Australia. A publicity leaflet has been found.

Volume 3

Pinder Bourne Designs (p8)
The Botanist character has been found superimposed on a blossom design.

Baby Plate (p12)
The two baby plates which were illustrated from the pattern books have now been found.

Gnomes (p27)
Group A: A baby plate has been discovered in this series.

Gnomes (p28)
Group B: Scene 4 has been found on a
sandwich plate, part of an unusual set
with a silver carrying stand enamelled
in the Gnomes design. A publicity
leaflet has been found.

Mermaids (p35)
A Baron jug with Holbein glaze has been found in this pattern which was illustrated previously from the pattern books.

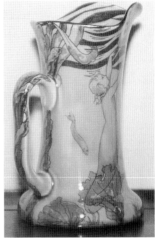

Aesthetic Style Maidens (p47)
Scenes 4, 6, 8, 9, 10 and 13 have now been found in this series, dated 1886 & 7, together with a new scene of a seated maiden holding out a bunch of flowers.

Aesthetic Style Maidens

Dancing Piccaninnies (p58)
This series has been found on a tobacco jar, not an ashtray as stated in the Appendix to Volume 4 (not illustrated).

Blue Children (p51)
Two more artist's signatures have been found on this series, L. Bentley and J. Hancock (not illustrated).

Cricketers - The All Black Team (p56)
Scene 3 'Out for a Duck' has been discovered in this series.

Sampler or Peter Pan (p73)
A round salad bowl has come to light in this design, showing a different scene.

Nursery Rhymes (p83)
Group A - Savage Cooper: A new scene has come to light featuring Little Jack Horner.

Springtime (p76)
A new scene has been discovered on a Dutch candlestick.

Nursery Rhymes (p89)
Group E: My Pretty Maid. A plate, featuring scene 3, has been discovered.

Nursery Rhymes (p86)
Group C: Scenes 1, 'Baa Baa Black Sheep' and 11, 'Simple Simon', have been found on a cream jug and sugar bowl.

Christmas - Santa Claus (p102)
A small teaset has been recorded in this series (not illustrated).

Snowflake (p105)
Perfume bottles and sprays featuring this
design with a Holbein glaze were made for
the Mignon company of New York in 1925.
The same shape has been found in a salt
and pepper set with metal tops.

Miniatures (p107)
Several more series have been
found in miniature:

Autumn Glory (vol 4)
Bayeux Tapestry (vol 1)
Blue Children (vol 3)
Country Garden (vol 2)
Countryside (vol 2)
Fisherfolk, Brittany (vol 4)
Flower Market (vol 4)
Game Birds (vol 4)
Hunting, Simpson (vol 2)
Kookaburra (vol 4)
Lincoln Imp (vol 1)
Old Moreton Hall (vol 1)

Pansies (vol 4)
Persian (vol 4)
Pipes of Pan (vol 4)
Ploughing (vol 2)
Poplars at Sunset (vol 4)
Prunus (vol 4)
Sampler (vol 3)
Souter (vol 1)
Tunis (vol 4)
Venice A (vol 4)
Woodland (vol 4)
Woodley Dale (vol 4)

Also the following miscellaneous scenes have
been recorded. Flambé country scene, blue
and white scenes of an owl, a hare and a pig.

Volume 4

Egyptian A (p20)
A bulb bowl with a Titanian glaze, inscribed
'Tutankhamen's Treasures, Luxor', has been
found in this series with the pattern number,
D4163 (not illustrated).

Greek (p30)
Group C: A new scene has been found on a
Concord jug.

Isthmian Games (p34)
Scene 1 has been found on a Tavern jug.

Australian Crests (p38)
Four new Crests have been recorded: Scotch
College (post 1921) on a tobacco jar; St.
Andrew's College, NSW, on a jug; Collegiate
School of St. Peter's, SA, on a jug; Prince
Alfred College, SA, on a teapot (not
illustrated).

Wattle (p43)
Group B: A new pattern number has been
recorded, D6212, and the wattle border has
been found with a goat design (not
illustrated).

Scene 8 has been found on an Athens teapot.

Gum Trees (p52)
Group A: A new scene has been discovered on a plate.

Polar Bears (p62)
A Poyntz jug has been found showing the trees background.

Dutch (p65)
Group A - Harlem: A keen collector has recorded many more scenes for the Dutch series.

36: Profile view of two young women carrying baskets with skirts billowing in the wind.

38: Three women walking together, arm in arm.

37: Two men, one with a book, talking to a woman with an umbrella.

39: Young girl and woman with a basket on her back, walking.

Dutch (p65)

40: Man standing with a walking-stick in one hand and basket in the other.

43: Woman walking with basket on her left arm.

41: Profile view of youth with his hands behind back.

44: Young man leaning backwards with stick over his right shoulder.

42: Man standing with his left hand on hip.

45: Woman and girl walking, carrying baskets.
46: Rear view of young woman.
47: Rear view of two women carrying baskets with skirts billowing in the wind.

Dutch

48: Two women and a young girl with hands on her hips.

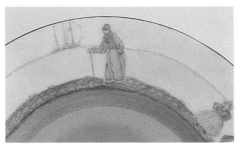

49: Man with stick in his right hand and left hand in pocket.

50: Rear view of two young girls.

51: Man with stick and fishing nets over his right shoulder.

52: Front view of man with his hands in pockets.

53: Old man with his hands in pockets.

54: Young man with oar over his left shoulder with basket in right hand.

Dutch (p65)

Group A: The following shapes have also been recorded in the Dutch series: Vase numbers 6869, 6905, 6921, 6923, 6924, 6928, 6930, 6999, 7000, 7002, 7005, 7007, 7383, and a shaped plate plus a beaker and comport made specially for Liberty's department store in London.

Dutch Flower Girls (p74)
A plate, depicting scene 7, has been found in this series.

Snowscenes A (p86)
Two new scenes have been discovered on a chamber pot and a vase.

Dutch (p70)

Group B: Ruysdael. An Aubrey toilet set jug, pattern number D2081, has been found depicting scene 1 from this series.

Group C: More characters have been recorded in this series: Man, side view, with hands behind back. Man, three-quarters view with hands in pockets (not illustrated).

Group E: A Ball teapot and stand have been found in this series.

Troika (p88)
A new scene has been discovered on an
octagonal plate.

Coat of Arms (p94)
'Utrium horum mavis accipe' is better
translated as 'take whichever you prefer'.
Different borders have also been recorded,
Grotesque, Band and Scroll (not
illustrated).

Historical Britain (p95)
This series has been seen with the
photographs coloured (not illustrated).

Old English Proverbs (p97)
A Flagon jug in Whieldon ware has been
found this series.

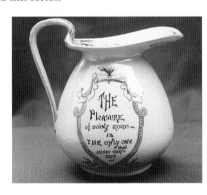

Venice A (p89)
A cup, saucer and tea plate have been found
featuring scenes previously illustrated from
the pattern book.

Prince Frederick (p99)
King George I has been found on a Tudor jug in the same style as Prince Frederick.

Moorish Gateway or Tunis (p108)
Two new scenes have been discovered: a woman playing a musical instrument in a gateway and a front view of a man with a donkey walking through the archway.

Arabs and Camels A (p102)
A new scene has been discovered on a plate.

New Zealand Crests (p114)

The crest of Rotorua has been recorded on a plate (not illustrated).

American Buildings (p128)

Group C: A new scene, Pike's Peak, has been recorded in this series with a Band and Scroll border (not illustrated).
Group D: A jug has been found depicting the Longfellow Mansion.

Mason's Lodge Centenary (p131)

A Tankard jug has been found featuring the Ancient Landmark Lodge no.17.

Bermuda A (p132)

Three Bermuda scenes have been wrongly attributed to the Australian Views A series and they include scene A6 and two unidentified scenes previously illustrated on p46 of Volume 4.

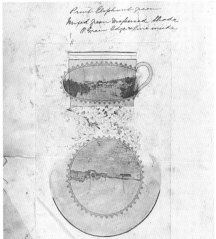

Dogs and Game A (p138)

A new scene has been found featuring the boar on its own and another featuring a dog and fox (not illustrated).

Farm Animals (p140)

Group A: The designer of this series was S. Wilson (not illustrated).

Heraldic and Grotesque Animals A (p143)

A new quotation has been recorded on a cats jug 'May we never crack a joke to break a reputation', D2454 (not illustrated).

Bewick Birds (p147)

A new scene, featuring two ducks, has been recorded (not illustrated).

Bird of Paradise A(p148)
A rack plate and vase number 7352 can now be illustrated in this series.

Crows (p150)
Group A: This design was used on an unusual Cadogan teapot.

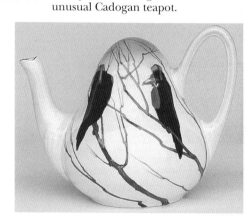

Game Birds B (p155)
A new scene has been found on a plate featuring a sandpiper.

Léonce Birds (p159)
A plate, depicting scene 3, has been found with pattern number D2071, which now dates the series introduction to 1904. The same number is found on the Bewick Birds series (not illustrated).

Mythical Bird B (p160)
Two plates have now been found in this series, one is decorated in shades of brown, red and yellow; the other in blue, red and yellow.

Penguins A (p162)
A Nimrod teapot, teapot stand, cream jug, sugar bowl and a Poyntz jug have been discovered in this rare series.

Persian A (p163)
A bone china plate has been recorded, dated 1935, which indicates that the pattern was not withdrawn during World War I as previously thought (not illustrated).

Fish (p175)
More species of fish have been recorded in this series, Bream, D4757, and Murray Cod, D4779 (not illustrated).

Oceana (p179)
This pattern has been found on a most unusual basin fitting and soap holder dated 1897.

Floral Patterns (p181)
An unusual plate has been found similar to Floral Patterns I but with an embossed white centre. A plate has now been found in group R.

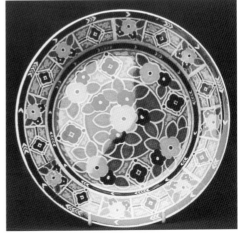

Anemones A (p188)
A vase has been found in this series
which was previously illustrated from a
publicity photograph.

Hollyhocks (p194)
This pattern should be
described as Delphiniums
(not illustrated).

**Flowers and Fruit on
Mottled Background** (p193)
Scene 5 has been found on a tray.

Prunus B (p199)
A teapot has been found in this series
which was illustrated previously from the
pattern books.
An unusual candlestick, shape 7795, has
also been recorded (not illustrated).

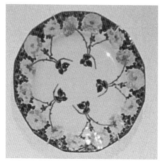

Roses B (p200)
A rack plate has been
discovered in this series.

Sweet Peas (p203)
A rack plate has been discovered
in this series.

Apples (p205)
An example of this design has been recorded with the title Nature (not illustrated).

Pollards (p211)
This series has been found on a bone china body (not illustrated).

Tulips C (p204)
A rack plate which was previously illustrated from the pattern books has been found in this series .

Trees (p212)
A vase and bowl have been found in the Trees A pattern which was illustrated previously from the pattern books. A Nimrod cream jug and sugar bowl have been found in Trees B - Deadwood Crackle.

Miscellaneous Patterns (p213)
Abstract
A bowl has been found with the pattern number D5082.

Riverside Views

A new scene, designed by Herbert Betteley, has been found on a Castle jug and Quorn biscuit barrel. Two pattern numbers have been recorded, D3300 and D4473 and these date the design to 1910.

Zodiac (p220)

Two series of 12 bone china plates featuring the signs of the Zodiac were produced between 1971 and 1975. The 10½ inch size was called a Birthday plate and features the individual sign surrounded by a Zodiac border. The 6¼ inch size, without the Zodiac border, was called a Lucky Zodiac plate.

Zodiac (p220)

A cup and saucer of this design, previously illustrated from the pattern books in the Appendix to Volume 4, has now come to light. It was known as an Egyptian Divining Cup and the design was registered in 1908.

Royal Bayreuth

The facsimile signature of Charles Noke, Art Director of Royal Doulton, has been found on items made by this German porcelain factory. The printed designs of Jesters (Volume 2, p13) are identical to the Royal Doulton examples and they have been found on a Bisley shape jug with a Royal Bayreuth backstamp. Other Royal Bayreuth shapes, which have been found with the Jesters pattern, are different in style to Royal Doulton shapes and include a wall pocket, candlestick and spill vase.

Royal Bayreuth

Royal Bayreuth also made versions of Blue Children ware (Volume 3, p51) and it may be that the company which produced the transfers for Royal Doulton also sold them to Royal Bayreuth. Whether Charles Noke was aware of the situation is not known.

A 19th century Staffordshire jug by an unknown maker has been found featuring the same scenes as in Royal Doulton's Greek B series (Volume 4, p26).

Some of the Welsh scenes have also been made by another company and a miniature perfume bottle has been recorded (Volume 2, p104).